I0697162

UNPAMPERED WISDOM

WISDOM FOR THE THICK-SKINNED INDIVIDUAL

BY

ENDALL BEALL

Imprint: Independently published

DEDICATION

This book is dedicated to those with the courage to handle frank speech in a world of emotionally domesticated egos.

Table of Contents

Introduction

This book is filled with honest, frank and straightforward observations. It is, overall, a critique of human behavior based on what we believe to be reality. I challenge narratives for it is narratives that shape our beliefs and ultimately control our awareness. I have no sacred cows in these observations. Everything is a fair target.

There are probably things in this book that are going to piss off many readers because their beliefs get called on the carpet. Regardless of your personal emotional reaction to what is contained in these pages, I am only criticizing beliefs, not you personally because I don't know you. If you take personal affront at the observations I share, your emotional reactions are your issue to contend with, not mine. I have no control over your emotional reactions.

We presently live in a world where humanity has become so domesticated and filled with easy to offend nice-niks that frank speech has become anathema. For over a century since the Theosophical Society imported Eastern religions and sought to harmonize them with western thought, the West has been subjected to a form of psychological docilization.

We are presently involved in a psychological war of massive proportions and the battlefield is words and rhetoric.

Through the advancement of Theosophical doctrines which expanded to create the New Age Movement and the modern spirituality movement, its followers have been turned into overly sensitive pushovers whose greatest insult to a differing frank observation is to call them 'negative'. This same mindset has permeated public thought since the introduction of Political Correctness in the 1990s. Where before, this verbal docility was more prevalent in liberal or left-leaning spiritual ideologies, it has now spread across the spectrum where every petty ego is looking to be offended at anything that doesn't agree with them or their ideological beliefs. The latest example found in the censorship of 'wokeness' is the expected result of bruised human egos wanting to censor anything that disagrees with their personal belief biases. The greatest casualty in all this is the loss of frank honesty and plainspeak. The world is willfully blinding and deafening itself through this process of psychological self-censorship and overdriven ego pettiness.

Everyone finds themselves tiptoeing around everyone else's emotions to avoid the backlash from butthurt egos just waiting on the chance to put on their victimhood badge and scream about how offended they are over your alleged 'negativity'. This is not just a left-wing issue, the victim cum offended mentality poison permeates our world. This has created a psychosis of self-censorship where people fear speaking their minds out of the emotional reactive retribution from those always looking for offense. I refuse to play this game of verbal paranoia, and so should you.

There is a distinction between frank observations and dancing around the flowered bordering of words just to make someone's petty ego keep from exploding and dumping their verbal vitriol on you for doing so. It has created a world of psychotic, infantile and inhuman behavior. I don't care about petty and needy victimized egos. I don't care about your hurt feelings. Your emotions are your problem, not mine. As such, I refuse to cater to such victim mentality and nurture or enable your psychosis. If you can't handle franks truth and observations, you are part of the problem, not the solution.

I am a strong advocate for the advancement of human consciousness, and the observations in this book are geared for that purpose, no matter how critical they may seem. Humanity has been coaxed along to advance its awareness for over 2,500 years with doctrines of compassion and love, yet none of its doctrine promoters over the ages can put their money where their mouth is. They talk one way and act another. It is obvious that pampering humanity with such doctrines of docility is an utter failure. With the domesticated and docile sensibilities present in the modern world, it's time someone takes the pacifier out of the baby's mouth and bitch-slaps that portion of humanity who can pull themselves out of this docility tailspin to grow up and wake up. Perhaps this material will get through to some of you. I make no apologies for your hurt feelings. Maybe they should be hurt to awaken you from your programmed slumber and laziness waiting on some supernatural agent to fix the problems humanity created for itself.

This pernicious form of psychological warfare has gone unnoticed because it caters to one's emotional desire to feel good.

Because these ideologies make their believers feel good, or feel that they have an exclusive free pass to heaven for nothing more than professing their beliefs, it has created not only a sense of insufferable arrogance in the believers in all these ideologies, but a sense of cosmic entitlement. This same sense of entitlement has morphed its way into the materialist religion of Marxism and is patently obvious with so many people demanding everything for free – naturally paid for by the government, which only functions on the tax dollars coerced from the public. The sense of victimhood and entitlement runs the spectrum of human expectations at this point of our sordid species evolution. With these facts in mind, I feel I have set the stage for what follows. Enjoy the journey!

Everything Else. . . .

Welcome to the narrative controlled matrix that rules human herd awareness.

Repeated tradition is repetitive multi-generational programming. It is a method of continually dragging the past around with us and never growing beyond the baggage it weighs us down with. One cannot create themselves anew if they are only walking shadows of the past. This is humanity's curse.

With an unchanging past the future will always be written to its tune and its outcome will always be predictable. The future is a continuing faulty past repeated and relived. Humanity refuses to break this programming and therefore continues to repeat the same mistakes over and over again. never growing, never changing, always staying stuck in the bag of the past. This, we call stability, normalcy or tradition.

Humanity doesn't want solutions; it only wants conflict and drama.

Humans continue to deny the truth, even when it is revealed. They only want 'truth' that supports their narrative reality, not the real truth.

Narratives are not truth; they are only stories that people believe to shape their perceptual realities. Every religion, ideology and 'ism' is only a trap for human awareness - stories that negatively enchant the mind and emotions to control the human herds. This is the real black magic that poisons humanity - living in a world of continual storybook illusions and people are simply too afraid to challenge and let go of their reliance on these stories because they shape who they are. Destroy the story and you destroy the false personality that is identified by the story itself. This is the real Matrix - the mind poison that dooms humanity so long as it demands to perpetuate the storybook reality they live.

Wisdom has no value in today's world. What most consider wisdom to be is simply conformity of ideology. Conventional wisdom is not wisdom, it is only herd agreement.

You cannot penetrate the armor of a closed mind.

To be on the defensive, one must first be a victim. To be offended, one must first feel victimized.

Just because you don't believe something doesn't make it untrue. Just because you do believe something doesn't make it true. Everyone has their perceptual barriers and their walls of illusion that they protect like a mama bear. Whatever feeds your perceptual and emotional comfort zone is what shapes your reality - nothing more. The narrative illusion rules. Programmed acceptance keeps the illusion in place.

Humanity doesn't want the hard answers, the truthful answers, it wants the simple answers delivered in as short a form as possible in a black and white format so people can determine points of conflict only. If the answer isn't simple, their dumbed down brain programming can't process the data.

It is pointless to provide edifying information to a species that has no desire to edify itself. Wallowing in the swill of cognitive squalor is more appealing to arrogant, rigid know-it-alls.

You cannot pierce the armor of arrogant human ignorance. The overinflated ego thrives in such an environment. protecting its own sense of self-superiority regardless of how facts cast shade on its personal illusions.

It is interesting when we see the linkage of cults and mind control. It is more interesting to see how when cults get mainstream recognition as religions they are no longer considered cults as they were in their infancy, but the mind control only deepens and ossifies once it is culturally codified and becomes institutionalized.

The human ego is a blustering, chickenshit bullshit artist. It protects the lies of its narrative beliefs because these beliefs form its shallow identity. The ego is a thin-skinned self-deceiver that claims to want one thing then totally shuns what doesn't conform to its narrative reality. The ego is an inveterate liar, and everyone buys their own ego's bullshit all too much.

The ego cannot grow, although it can and does over-inflate itself to the edification of the ego-driven human. It professes ideologies of love but doesn't hesitate to hate anything that disrupts its self-delusion. It is a program of contradictions that can only function through excuse-making rationalizations and uses little real rationale or logic to support its own delusions. Things don't have to make sense to the ego, they only need to make it feel potent to justify all its psychoses.

"I'll prove you wrong!" can be a powerful motivator on the road to unraveling the lies of illusion so long as one is sincere in the research efforts it can lead to. Simply saying, "Oh yeah, well my belief says different" is not proving anything wrong and will lead nowhere. It only leaves one stuck in place, unchanging and unmoving. Confirmation bias does not reveal truth, it just more strongly embeds pre-existent programming and proves nothing.

The common man has no capacity to rule themselves. In this matter they are wholly incompetent. History proves this. The common man is only a mob. Fact.

Humanity has yet to learn about freedom without constraints and restrictions based on ownership of self and personal responsibility. Every concept of freedom humanity presently exhibits is limited freedom controlled by laws and presumed holy mandates used to regulate behavior because mankind has not yet learned the discipline to behave itself and mind its own business.

The true visionary is always the heretic of their times. Their view is farther down the road than the next few years into future decades, centuries or eons, and they are rarely appreciated, nor their visions accepted until a century or more after their death. It takes humanity this long at a minimum to catch up to their visions. Nothing has changed today with the staid status quo human herds who can only cling to the past with a white-knuckled tenacity, ever refusing to change in an ever-changing creation.

Can you think beyond the single God Creator narrative? Can you perceive anything different than the given narrative? Can you perceive something more than considering yourself a 'lesser being'?

I think it is funny watching Christians screaming about virtue signaling on the left since the entire religion has been virtue signaling from its inception. Gotta love the selective blindness irony of it all. Pots calling the kettle black.

Perhaps one day humans will want to be inquisitive instead of argumentative. When that happens, if it happens, perhaps this species will advance. As it stands, being argumentative is the preference and it shuts down the inquisitive nature.

You cannot provide deep principles to shallow minds.

Dismiss everything that is false, whether it insults your soul or not. Just because it makes you feel good doesn't mean it is valid.

Magical healings, miracles and raising the dead. In any other context this would be laughed out or considered occult, but if Jesus did it, hey, that's okay. One is amazed at the hoops of rationalization people jump through to justify their beliefs.

There is always choice and humans continually seem to make the wrong ones by and large.

There is no Devil except in the fearful and over-imaginative superstitious human mind. But it is a great mind-control narrative that unfortunately works only too well.

I wonder how long it will be before the illusion of reality unravels enough that people become ready to accept viable alternative explanations about why their fragile reality is crumbling and what to do in the aftermath of that dissolution?

Would that humans would direct their focus on expanding their consciousness as much as they worry about their bodies. The greatest plague infecting humanity is ignorance and the arrogance thinking one knows more than what they do. Humanity's ailments are more emotionally and psychologically oriented. What humanity needs to heal is its mind, which will lead to bodily improvements in time. Healthy bodies don't count for much inhabited by stupid minds. They are just grunt labor.

One cannot contain consciousness, nor should one try, yet humans insistently demand that consciousness fits into their limited cognitive belief boxes. They want consciousness to conform to their petty ego desires rather than setting these boxes of control aside and meeting consciousness on the broader turf of understanding.

While many have spent perhaps decades chasing this phantom called consciousness and sought to make it conform to their ideas of what they think it should be, they keep missing the boat, seldom reaching much understanding in the process. They have accepted stories about spirituality, yet consciousness is not spiritual, it is merely consciousness. It needs no definition, for to define it only keeps it away from one wanting to experience it. You can't hold the ocean in a teacup, you have to toss the cup to become part of the ocean, otherwise you are merely a teacup thinking it is the ocean.

Everything is not Satanic sacrifice. Human stupidity plays a large factor in many of these things. People really need to pull their heads out of their asses by constantly blaming every stupid human act on Satan. You look like superstitious idiots.

The discomfort of growth comes when we have to face down the illusions we embrace as reality. The more one deprograms themselves from the illusion, the more painful the process is, yet it lessens over time as one evolves into seeing through the illusions and can more easily let the old programming go in favor of more beneficial insights.

"We hold these truths to be self-evident, that all men are created equal. . . "

This means that all men are born of women, that is their equality. After that, all bets are off in the equality dept. Each individual's aspirations and what they achieve in life is predicated upon their personal motivation and self-determination. This is the "Life, Liberty and pursuit of Happiness" which everyone is allowed. This doesn't mean that that Liberty is to be constrained by groupthink in any fashion or through psychological coercion. Groupthink in any capacity is the 'equalizer' that reduces all men and women to nothing more than slaves to a narrative and mob coercion. Groupthink is anathema to true individual freedom. Every narrative spawns collectivist groupthink and demands conformity to its ideology. Ponder this and see.

There is a psychosis in an ideology that promotes suffering as its measure of value. It is a perpetual victim mentality.

I await the day to see the common man elevates himself to become an uncommon man. Nah, probably not going to happen, never has. Plodding along the same as ever is much easier and less challenging. That is why the common man stays common, no motivation to become something more.

The big question no one seems to be able to answer:

Regardless of which doctrinal ideology people adhere to, going to heaven forever and ever; magically waking up on a new parallel Earth or Ascending to the 5th dimension or becoming multidimensional (however you may imagine what that means), we always come down to the seminal question no one seems to have the wisdom to ask. What is this question?

Then what?

You see, everyone thinks of all these things as a goal, as a reward, as some kind of end game, but no one ever seems to consider or particularly answer 'Then what'? Therefore, I am asking any all takers to this challenge to tell me, from their own perspective, that if you get what your beliefs tell you and are expecting and aching for, then what? This is not a baiting question, it is a sincere inquiry to see who has ever thought it through enough to get beyond the reward/expectation promises of the ideologies you believe.

The majority is not the concern, you will never convince the majority, and that is the error in human thinking - trying to wake up the herds. You only need to waken those who have the desire to be so. Backwards looking is an always fail. Getting stuck in ancient traditions just because they are old is a fail. This is why people who claim to be on a 'spiritual' quest are not moving forward very fast, if at all. They are stuck trying to use the old to understand a new and more dynamic paradigm.

Humanity's perceptions are ruled by the false idea that concepts that were good for older generations apply to this and future generations. Consciousness is designed to evolve, not sit still, yet those who hang on to past traditions with a stranglehold will be the ultimate losers on the road to cognitive advancement. New times beget new ideas. Those who refuse to entertain new and challenging concepts doom themselves to repeating error. One cannot advance constantly dragging the past around with them like a ball and chain.

New concepts are always a challenge and rarely comfortable to consider when one is stuck in their stability rut. Those who demand to stay the same will not advance.

Some of the most educated people are the most blind and pigheaded.

You are never going to understand the Actuality only working through physical means and measurements. This is the failure within the religion of materialist scientism.

Make no mistake, materialist scientism is its own religion. It guards its precincts as rabidly as any religion protects its dogma.

All religions practice virtue signaling. That is how they convince their followers that they are the 'elect' or the chosen ones. When you can brainwash a herd of people to believe such nonsense you can control them. This is why I say that religion is the greatest mind control weapon ever developed - all religions, including the religions of Marx and Science.

The human Flesh Robot is a complex device. You have the bodymind and you have the intellect brain processor. These two aspects of 'mind' are often not in alignment, which causes much of the conflict he is talking about. The cure is not happiness and love, but attaining emotional equanimity or peace, what many call balance. This state of emotional and cognitive equanimity is what Buddha referred to as Nirvana. It is not a place, it is a state of cognitive healthiness where one can live comfortably within their own skin without all the reactive emotional disruption caused by these buried traumas.

What defines herd 'sanity' is highly questionable. The 'eccentric' original thinker/heretic is where the solutions are usually found, not within the herd masses and groupthink.

There is a separation taking place between those who will choose to grow and those who won't. You will never wake up the masses, you can only awaken and advance yourself. Agonizing over the complacency of the herd will only hold you back in your own advancement. You are not humanity's daddy or babysitter. You can move no one who doesn't choose to move themselves, you can only hold yourself back by fretting over their refusal to grow. It is tragic to observe, but moving beyond letting the herd's recalcitrance hold you back will be to your best personal benefit toward higher consciousness understanding and wisdom. The first key piece of wisdom you can learn is that you only have jurisdiction within your own skin. You have no authority over others, you can only provide information if you choose. It is up to them to do or not do regarding what that information may present. This is one of the hardest things we have to learn on this road to advancement, that others are responsible for themselves. You are only responsible for you where your cognitive growth is concerned. Herd indoctrination and 'greater good' thinking is an impediment, not an advantage to personal growth. Breaking herd programming is a bitch, but it can be accomplished.

The first hurdle I will challenge you with is that spirit as humans perceive it does not exist, it is consciousness. Humans perceive spirit to be their soul, which is just an extension of their ego personality into infinity. It is a major ego insecurity. The process is more complex than dumb human egos living forever because they profess a specific belief. The belief doesn't matter to consciousness, which lives on before and after human physical life. Because humans don't understand the process of life they live in fear because of that ignorance. They do not understand why humans were created or our purpose for being here. I have explained much of this in my books and it has been explained in a different format (saying the same thing) in other works publicly available. The sad fact is that no one seems to want to listen, but instead choose to compartmentalize knowledge into their narrow perception boxes they call reality. One cannot expand if they continually contract and compress the information into what they think they know. There is no growth in doing so.

With so many people on the so-called spiritual path, talking about a shift in consciousness, I wonder how many have even considered what they are really seeking beyond their supernatural fantasies on the subject.

You see, people gravitate to certain narratives, all designed to literally enchant their imaginations, usually with fanciful folderol, and that is what they think they are looking for. But cognitive advancement is really none of those things. They are magical expectations for the most part. Even if one does have experience that goes beyond the accepted norm, they translate it through their narrative filters and belief structure, often missing the true nature of what occurred.

People fear the unknown. That is the problem, they don't know how to embrace it. To embrace the unknown, one must become a genuine creator. One will never be a creator while following someone else's script.

The bad thing is that people often consider a point of view that differs from or challenges their comfortable belief paradigm as rudeness. They also call it 'negativity' because the ideas disrupt their comfort zone. This is neither rude nor negative, it is meant to be educational for those who genuinely seek to know more than what they think. One will never advance while they are parked and in idle.

Affirmations don't do much good, it is only the ego lying to itself.

Humanity's world is built on illusion, Even the concept of being in the now is an illusion because by the time you figure out it is the now it has become the past.

This is how slaves think - Give me a new master, maybe he will be nicer.

To fit into a human herd - If you agree with their dogma, whatever it is, you'll be fine.

The herds detest difference, they demand conformity.

The common man has never had any power except as an unruly mob. Humans can't generally behave themselves without the threat of punishment to make them do so. To expect them to work together under self-rule is impracticable at this stage of human cognitive development. Everyone wants a daddy, whether it is God or the State and few if any can even govern themselves.

The only evil is tyranny. There is no crime, no foul deed you can name that doesn't have its roots in tyranny, whether it is the few tyrannizing the many or individuals tyrannizing one another either through physical or psychological intimidation. There may be many reasons why humans tyrannize one another, it can't all be boiled down to greed or the quest for political power but is more often just the human ego wanting to get its way. Every human being is their own petty tyrant, yet nary a one will admit this or seek to change it within themselves. It is always 'the other guy' that is the tyrant, 'not me!' The ego owns nothing of its own actions on a deeper psychological or emotional level, it only blames others.

Until people can see the tyrant that lies within and cease being one, nothing will change.

Being chosen is not all it's cracked up to be.

Every ideology, every religion is herd collectivism. The individual is always lost under herd ideological narrative control. I am against all such ideologies and in favor of the responsible individual, of which there seem to be very few humans.

Believing is there for those who don't 'know'.

Show me a live action un-retouched photo of this Satan character or shut the fuck up with your supernatural hobgoblining.

The written word was designed to enslave humanity, not free it.

Consciousness precedes matter.

No religion is rational, including the religion of Marx.

Hope was an evil that Pandora found in the box. It is an addictive substance.

Every human avoids facing the truth of themselves, lying to themselves about themselves continually.

Consciousness only works through biological interface. Mechanical AI will never achieve it.

Do we all need salvation from our humanity because the Christian God did such a fucked-up job designing us?

Humans think too much, that is humanity's bane. Humans need to stop thinking and start perceiving. There is a profound difference.

The entire human species is not only addicted to fear; it is addicted to supernaturalism as the answer to its fears.

All of humanity is disharmonic. They all love hating 'the other' too much to mature out of their hatred and paranoia.

Eventually all religions will pass once they are seen through and understood. Most don't want to know, they love supernaturalism, guilt, shame, virtue signaling and blame-laying too much to let go.

Churches have always rejected truth. Peddling a belief in a fictional devil is all the proof one needs to see that.

There is no devil except in the fearful and over-imaginative superstitious human mind. But it is a great mind-control narrative that unfortunately works only too well.

Every human ego must have its bragging points to edify itself.

Get rid of the psychopaths and sociopaths and all you have left is human idiots who can't rule themselves. They can only fight each other looking to be offended all the time. In this environment, there is no solution except to remedy human ignorance, and I don't see that happening any time soon.

People don't know any real history which is why they learn nothing from it. They have been fed sanitized and propagandized narrative kool-aid for so long that they love the multiple flavors of the lies they embrace.

Humanity hasn't learned shit in its long enslavement regarding human behavior. They are still the dumb assholes they always were despite their technological gadget advancement.

Humans filthied up the planet, it is their responsibility to clean up their own shit. Stop begging God to do it for you,

----

Christianity has run its own brand of cancel culture for centuries. How it sucks when the tide turns, eh?

Humanity's greatest yoke of bondage is the psychological dependency on narratives created by others to control and domesticate them.

Why do people always expect wisdom from figureheads and never a common 'peer'? Was Jesus an authority figure, or Buddha in their time? It amazes me how controlled by the 'obedience to authority syndrome' this species is, but the basis of it goes back to the creation of this slave species. The 'authorities' have NEVER provided humanity with real wisdom, only their exceptional fellow men. Authority figures provide intellectualist fodder, not wisdom. Actors above all, people who pretend to be other people to make a living, should never be sought as a source of any kind of genuine wisdom.

It is a plague on humanity. The entire world lives on being offended by something or someone. That is why it is bordering on species suicide. Hate the other has been the mantra of human history.

He who seeks to be offended never listens, he only seeks reason to be offended.

Life at present is a perceptual narrative illusion and human beings are just the dumb characters keeping it alive.

I prefer a broader perspective than a single insecure God that expects worship and fawning from his followers, his 'servants'. By any other name a servant is a slave and I have transcended the slave mentality that all religions promote, including the religion of Marx. I much prefer freedom to submission.

Great, just what we need, a heaven filled with stupid humans. I'll pass, thank you.

People need to grow the motivation to light and keep their own candle burning. Anything else is welfare mentality for the weak.

The human ego is driven by the thinking mind, which in most of us never ceases to stop thinking all the damn time. The false ego self is that part of us that uses narratives and beliefs to shape and identify who we THINK we are. This false ego is but a character in someone else's play, it is not the real you who needs no attachment to these continual narrative dramas. I know this sounds hard to comprehend, yet it is our attachment to and the defense of these narratives that prevents us from accessing the consciousness network of the Actuality. Because of the constantly thinking mind and the false ego personality that identifies with these beliefs, we block ourselves from this network of awareness.

Aside from defending the narratives that shape who we are, we are constantly defending this false ego-self built around all these beliefs, ever looking for slight or insult to preserve this false self-image. Consciousness works through insight and intuition, not through thinking. You will never THINK your way to consciousness, you will merely be conscious, and there is a distinction. Being conscious means your intellect is aware of its surroundings and the human body. Consciousness is not physical, and with the human fixation on the body and the dramas that we constantly engage in through the conflict of narratives, we blockade the silence we need to intuit and 'feel' in a more subtle sensory capacity. The thinking brain never shuts up in its thinking echo chamber of self-doubt, worry, second guessing ourselves, guilt, shame and self-recrimination. The thinking brain constantly runs us in circles over these issues and more. To advance into awareness, as I have written for years, one has to stop THINKING like a human and expand beyond this useless process. The more you diminish yourself believing that you are a lesser being, that there is something higher than you, or that you are not connected to and function within the Actuality Field, you keep yourself cut off from what you seek to experience and know. It is the thinking brain, blinded by reactive emotions that prevent you from knowing what you desire. This applies to everyone.

Stop worrying about the herd. You can only do for yourself. The herd is not your problem and never has been. The sooner you can see this the sooner you will find your own peace of mind. You owe them nothing.

Humans have always been zoo animals, experimental cattle, but their egos refuse to admit this truth and free their minds from the control mechanism of the narrative state. They are each and all just characters reinforcing and defending someone else's narrative. They barely merit the title of walk-ons in the theater of life. They are ready-made drones to tyranny, it is all they have ever known - the bent knee to authority, whether God or government.

People won't admit they are conditioned. That is why their minds are shut tighter than a bear trap. They have to admit they are wrong, and the ego refuses to do this in its sublime sense of arrogance and pride.

No one will be judged in the afterlife, it is a cognitive salve thinking that some supernatural force or invisible being is going to make someone pay for their crimes after they are dead. Works great, idiots still believe this nonsense. It alleviates them taking responsibility for stopping the tyrants while they live.

The epiphany is that all humanity is insane.

A shaman 'guides' if he is worth his salt. He is not a hand-holder for those who don't have the courage to do their own work.

Every social network flocked to by the herds will be the same. They all move to what gratifies their ego programming the most. Flesh robots, all programmed by themselves to be the assholes that they are. I don't see a Christian tyranny as any better than a communist one, for it is all tyranny wrapped in ego self-justification.

The only thing that must change is human awareness, yet humanity refuses to let go of the illusions to advance its awareness. They want everything in a neat little cognitive box which they refuse to tear down or transcend. Continued refusal to do so only spells species demise. The Earth will endure, it is humanity' survival that is questionable.

'Equality' always settles at the bottom rung of the ladder.

Is calling a spade a spade being the bad guy? I detest all herd ideologies equally, Christianity in its 40,000 varieties, Islam, institutional Buddhism. Hinduism, Marxism - they are all just different foods for the herd beast mentality to feed their egos with. The lunacy is all equal in my eyes, and yes, I have outgrown it all. You could too but I doubt you have the courage to do so. It's much easier to be a slave and defend what enslaves you than to question it and free your mind.

Human idiocy and slave mentality is the only thing that bothers me, coupled with denied victimhood and the feeling of being unworthy. Stay a slave to your doctrine. No skin off my ass. Just stop playing the tyrant trying to shove your ideology down everyone else's throat for your conformity of thought narrative herd. It defies freedom.

Try to stop being a groveling slave weeping for status in the hereafter. You people and your immortality addiction are fucking pathetic to behold. You don't deserve the human life you forsake, chasing such hollow promises. You have been given a great gift called life but sneer at it in trade for afterlife promises. That is called buying a pig in a poke,

----

I am not lost and therefore don't need a salvation narrative. Actually, neither do you, but you probably can't accept that.

People are all arguing over supremacy of ideological narratives concocted by others to control their minds and emotions, each and every one slaves to what others created for them to believe, to keep them ever divided, to never to join together to possess the one thing none of them have - freedom from defending their selective narratives.

There is creation beyond the simple concept of God - a collective of individuated consciousnesses, of which we are all a contributing part, except we cannot accept our role in it all but prefer to be slaves to alleged divine bullshit ideologies as servants of some God or higher principle. We refuse to own ourselves or understand anything beyond what we have been told to believe by ideological controllers

----

Tyranny. There is no evil you can name, no crime imaginable that doesn't start with tyranny. This is undeniable fact. All tyranny is trespass, and this species thrives on trespassing on one another constantly, ergo, they are all petty tyrants in their sense of ego superiority and superiority of narrative dogma.

"*We Can Crush Their Narrative*" - So say those controlled by narratives who deny they are only characters in the narratives created by others.

There is no divine. There is no holy. There is only consciousness, and consciousness *is* life.

All humanity has been mentally ill for tens of thousands of years. They are just too crazy to admit this truth, nor are they interested in the cure. They love feeding the disease too much to let it go.

Failure to know history always leads to repeating it. Denying history because it doesn't conform to your indoctrinated beliefs is equally as dangerous.

Peer review was the start of academic whitewashing and censorship starting with the Royal Society.

Christianity has thrived on fear porn and hopium from its inception. People are so blind.

The purpose of life that humans don't want to hear is that we were created human to BE human, to live life as we choose and experience what we choose. This is called freedom, but humans are perpetual trespassing tyrants who can't mind their own business and allow others the same freedoms they demand for themselves. Humans simply hate being human. They would rather be anywhere else or anything other than what they are. They hate life and can only yearn or beg for some kind of escapist mystical or supernatural utopia when they won't lift a finger to bring it about for themselves as we live and have the capability, if not the will, to create heaven on earth.

We live in a human created hell and exhibit zero motivation to change this, perpetually bowing to ideas of supernatural entities who somehow owe us something. It is a massive mystical entitlement mill with slovenly beggars crying to the heavens to bring changes they are unwilling to make for themselves. The meaning in life is what you make of it while you have it. Pissing it away for supernatural intervention only illustrates the fact that this species is unqualified to meet its design specs and gains more pleasure feeding on one another rather than sitting at the table and trying to work things out. It's not the green pieces of paper who are unhappy, it is human ingrates that do not appreciate the gift of life while they have it.

For God-touters - You challenge God not existing in my mind, why does God exist in yours? You see, this is a two-way street, it all doesn't run your way, as much as you believe it does.

What do you envision as your eternal potential?

Destroy the rich! - The standard diatribe of the common man against the landed aristocracy since ancient Rome and before. Humans don't change, their programming is too deeply embedded, and they refuse to change. Always ready to criticize and always short on solutions beyond maintaining whatever the present cultural status quo dictates. And who created the status quo, the common wind-up toys? Never. It has always been the elite intellectuals, the literate classes that wrote the narratives to control the common drones who walk in lockstep once they are converted to the new cultural norm. Today the drone can read and write compared to our illiterate ancestors, but they are still programmed with the victim mentality of the jealous and envious child.

The Great Awakening is far from complete, the journey for humanity has much further to go if it will take the responsibility to do so. Being partly awake is no different than hitting the snooze alarm and that is all humanity is doing. People are only waking up as far as it makes them comfortable to live under control of their narrative beliefs. They are very far from accepting the full truth of things. The narratives still rule humanity's mind. Anything less is only hopium addiction and wishful thinking.

Consciousness doesn't expand without a sense of inquisitiveness. But it also doesn't expand much when our interests drift too far into nothing but curiosities. People looking to be offended will always find offense. I challenge malarkey ideas, it is the individual who makes it personal. One's personal need to feel offended is their affair and not my concern. My mannerism may be blunt and to the point, but I am still only challenging ideas. It is the individual ego that makes the idea their personal turf to defend protect. When the ego pumps itself up to defend itself and launches unwarranted personal assaults, then I will respond to them individually, not because I have anything to defend (especially my ego) but because no one should stand for abuse through personal assault. It's trespass and I refuse to be trespassed upon by butthurt petty ego outbursts. I have nothing to defend ideologically, and therein lies the major difference between how we perceive. If you want to expand into consciousness you are going to have to learn to be less defensive and ego driven. Lesson number one. Take it or leave it.

On churches, mosques and temples - The world will be a better place when these eyesores are seen for the edifices of tyranny they represent.

One thing about religionists is that they are all insufferable egotistical assholes, including the religion of Marx. The only difference in any of them is the narrative that controls their mind that they defend in their cognitive blindness and ego sense of superiority. Perhaps you should look at your own inner mirror to see how you contribute to the problems of the day rather than thinking your shit doesn't stink. That would be a major step forward.

Gonna get really rough when religions are revealed as a major part of humanity's tyranny.

Perhaps you should try to think outside your brainwashed narrative and see more. Nothing more dangerous than rigid zealotry for any ideology. Freedom is not chaos or anarchy except to the rigidly mind-controlled ideological robot that demands to be controlled by someone else's rules.

I have nothing to defend. Can you say the same? Until you own yourself you will always be defending someone else's story.

I have nothing to sell you except yourself. If you are uninterested, stay a slave. No concern of mine.

You don't know what instigates human nature or the arrogance of the selective ego, which can only blame and lay guilt on those that disagree with their personal ideology - which is what shapes their perceptual arrogance. Try looking into your own mirror before looking into mine, or as Jesus said, 'Before taking the splinter from another's eye, remove the plank from your own'.

I live comfortably within my own skin. I doubt you can say the same with all your afterlife anxieties.

Humans on this planet have always been slaves since their creation. Good luck getting arrogant egos to accept this sordid fact.

Actually, there is only one version of you, and this is it. Parallel universes and replica you's make zero sense.

The shepherds have *always* been wolves. Humans just refuse to admit it.

People demand leaders of any kind, so they don't have to take responsibility for leading themselves collaboratively. They demand an authority because they are too lazy and hardheaded to learn how to get along together.

The herds have always been controlled by the minority elite. Humans don't know the reason for this and quickly discount the explanations because they refuse to truth in favor of the fictional narratives that control their minds.

Pull your head out of your ass, I think you don't need the instructions. Well, perhaps you do.

There is no God as you believe him to exist. Sorry. Recalibrate your programming.

Is it your reality or just one chosen from the menu of choices offered?

Why are so many people willing to die for a cause yet seemingly unwilling to live with the same fervor? Maybe people should consider what is wrong with this mindset.

The whole world is fooled in one fashion or another. Their eyes shut, their ears fill, and their brain goes into overdrive to protect their own favored deceiving narrative. You will *never* convince them otherwise because they all firmly believe *they* are the exception to this rule.

I have a problem with drones programmed by ideologies like wind-up toys, no matter what the doctrine is. They are all slaves to ideas not of their making. They are all sheep to someone else's slaughter, the flocks subjugating themselves to shepherds masquerading as God, whether that is a supernatural myth or the mythical State playing God. The herds will fight and die to defend these illusions and go to their graves thinking they will attain some glory in an afterlife that is also simply a myth. They will just be dead humans who died for nothing more than an idea sold to them by someone else, a belief.

If you look at those stars and believe we are all alone in the universe, you are a fool.

Stupidity has a price and fear makes idiots pay it.

True advancement comes when people realize the truth of 'everything is a lie' includes their most closely held beliefs. It's all or nothing, admitting that everything is a lie except the one you choose to embrace will only leave you enslaved to the world of lies and illusions. It's *all* a lie, as in *ALL*, not just the parts you don't like.

People are evil because they are assholes. No supernatural explanation is necessary to understand that. Humans just won't own their own responsibility in the matter. It's easier to blame a mythical creature than it is to accept responsibility for the actions of people. Why is this so hard to come to terms with?

People are just like looking for reasons to be offended. It boosts their ego and their self-righteousness.

I don't pity the fools; they don't deserve it for their self-enforced ignorance. Stupidity has a price, let them pay it and spare your emotions fretting over the idiots.

If people could learn to face and transcend their own shit they could deal with the other shit in a different manner.

Your perceptions are controlled by cultural narratives which are not your own.

Minding one's own business is about the last thing humans do. They are perpetual nosy busybodies who can't mind their own business, which lies at the root of humanity's problems and herd mentality.

There is no God there is nothing under his control except your mind and the myth, which are both controlled by you.

You are only slaves to a fictional narrative.

It is not the fall of humanity; it is humanity committing suicide through willful ignorance and reliance on some magical external force to fix it for them. Not going to happen.

People are supposed to be the change, not sit on their asses waiting for it to be given to them. It starts with changing yourself, which most are totally unwilling to do.

You don't know the names of the highest manipulators, only the superficial stooges.

There are numerous factors that contribute to religious thinking, some temporal and physical, others appear mystical because humanity couldn't expand beyond 3D thinking to perceive anything greater. The mystical aspect in itself is not easy to define, and part of the explanation, most people are unwilling to accept.

We live in a very convoluted experience machine I call The Actuality (I use the term machine very loosely here). It is about consciousness and its ongoing expansion and creation. Although there is a lot about us being co-creators circulating in the modern spiritual circus, most people only think about creating for their physical pleasure and ease and don't really grasp the magnitude of what that fully means. Like all things, these ideas are all intellect and emotion driven and therefore only cater to the ego. Folks are really going to have to ratchet up their game to perceive the larger scope of the Actuality. Science is sniffing around the edges but still missing the mark.

The concept of soul being equated with consciousness is also based on major misunderstanding; they are not the same. I find few who can actually stretch their perceptions to grasp the greater concepts of it all without reducing it to known human thinking.

This species doesn't understand nuance, it only groks 'in your face' reality. Trying to teach them nuance is like trying to teach your dog to piss in the toilet - i,e, wasted effort. The stupidity of this species is spelling its own demise. Hard to watch, but it is what it is.

The brain is only the data processor of the flesh robot and relied on way too much as it is.

Observing how the 'think positive and massage my hopium infected ego' plagues this species, I realize that people can't stand pragmatic observations about their ego self-image and its insufficiencies. 'Don't bust my bubble' is the cry of the satiated and comfortable flesh robot. Will we find a catalyst that will galvanize humanity into changing itself? I'm not sure that will happen. If what we have observed thus far in the so-called Great Awakening hasn't done so, then I am unsure what might.

I find it funny how ego-driven assholes ask what you have done when they have done nothing themselves except bluster and bleat like the sheep they are, idly parroting their memorized ideological platitudes think that counts as wisdom. They can't think of anything except how victimized they are - by the government, by happenstance, by God or the Devil, or evil aliens hounding us from space - to perceive anything beyond their known and heavily controlled world of perception. If you do tell them what you have done, they minimize it and disparage it because they are too inept to graduate beyond their mental enslavement. I give no thought to small-minded bellyachers who contribute to nothing but the polarized conflict. They are all self-made victims. Funny how the word 'negative' has become a protective mechanism for so many hopium addicts avoiding hard truths.

Everyone thinks. The problem resides in the limited ceiling of perception they operate within. Thinking with the brain processor is made the primary function when it should be a secondary function to ponder what we perceive otherwise. I have stated for some time now that we have to stop thinking like a human, meaning that we think all the time - what you think, what you thought, what you think you're going to think, and the brain processor never ever shuts up in that scenario. One will never be able to silence the mind to perceive differently so long and the thinking engine is engaged 24/7.

The picture is greater than the formulated destruction of the US. It is universal in scope and we are a young species living on a very small planet in the back woods of the Milky Way galaxy.

We are observing the collapse of a played out and worn out system of awareness in the process of being 'upgraded' to a broader and more expanded working system of awareness than what has carried us this far. Every human(oid) species across the cosmos is facing this same collapse/upgrade scenario that we are, although they don't all carry quite the same type of baggage this species drags around with it being created as a slave race that has never known true freedom.

People are fighting in one form or another to preserve this collapsing system, which may well lead to humanity's demise on this planet if we refuse to upgrade. Defending the old system in all its forms is doomed to failure, but humans have shown themselves to often not be the brightest bulb in the box. It remains to be seen whether we survive our own childhood or not. Right now, it looks pretty grim.

Buddhism is the only 'religion' on the planet that doesn't promote God. This is because Buddha was teaching about consciousness, not the slavery subservient worship. This is why the Hindu priesthoods of his time declared that all Buddhists must be killed. His teachings of pragmatism and expanding one's awareness was a direct threat to the institutions of godly dependency in India.

Christians won't admit it, but their teacher Emmanuel (who wasn't renamed Jesus until the religion creators came along) taught the same thing in his own fashion 500 years after Buddha. I covered these comparisons in my book From Belief to Truth - From Truth to Wisdom, if you are interested. Once again, his teachings threatened the status quo.

Before about 700 BC or thereafter, there was no concept of a heavenly afterlife. The idea of humans going to heaven, which had previously only been reserved to the gods, did not exist. All there was was life in the dreary underworld. As a transitory phase before the idea of humans going to heaven, the concept of a pain and illness free human afterlife developed in Egyptian religion and was also found in the idea of the Elysian Fields belief where the person would be joined by their loved ones in an idyllic afterlife -- but it wasn't heaven as people perceive it today. I covered this extensively in The Truth About the 'Divine' Soul.

There is a deeply ingrained program in the human psyche about the entire God thing, which will be briefly explained in my upcoming book Ancient History Unlocked (which should be uploaded today for publication) and which I explained in more depth in other volumes referenced in that book. Humanity's fixation on both God and immortality are intimately linked together. In other words, there is a pragmatic explanation for these hang-ups in human beings without having to resort to speculation and mysticism. One must accept a different explanation than what is presently available in the marketplace of ideas.

Humans are a very young species and they stand at the threshold of transcending that childhood - if they choose to. Our science and technology has give us a platform for greater understanding, but even materialist scientism is locked in its own small room of perceptual acceptance, little different than mystical or religious traditions. Again, I have written extensively on this as well in The Actuality and in The Actuality Field. The cosmos is like an ocean of consciousness and humanity wants to fit it into a teacup. To meet consciousness - enlightenment - one must get out of the teacup.

It's easy to observe, everything is corrupt except my belief system, so thinks the average human. It's called selective blindness.

How about we drop all the God shit and just be responsible co-creators? That should be enough, no?

There is no universal mind. There is however a single framework I call The Actuality in which all awareness functions, both physical and immaterial. One is not and cannot be separated from the Actuality unless they think they are, and even then, they are not separate, only self-deluded, which all of humanity presently is.

People don't know how predictably the same they really are.

Don't worry about the 'gonna doers', they can fend for themselves and do without for not doing and always putting things off. The world is filled with gonna doers. Tell them what's coming and what to focus on for months on end and they are always gonna do things but never do. I have written them off.

Everyone deserves what they get based on the narratives they accept as reality - no exceptions.

Humans can only mouth the words unconditional love. Everything the ego does and perceives is conditional.

Every human being is a flesh robot. The sooner people realize this the sooner they can accept the fact that the entire species is badly programmed robots - mostly faulty self-programming.

Hope, just another evil from Pandora's Box. Who listens and avoids this evil?

Everybody has to play the victim. This entire species is that way, a bunch of whining victims.

All humans play the blame game.

There is no Satan, that is a Christian myth used to drive superstitious and fearful people into the churches. It is the fear 'stick' that drives them to the 'carrot' of alleged salvation. Both concepts are lies, but they feed the ego and the emotions, and unfortunately, the psychological manipulation works all too well. Humans and human behavior - their utter inability to behave themselves - is the root cause and until humans own their own perfidious behaviors nothing will change. Humans create the problems; they must mature enough to see it and uncreate it. God is just an excuse not to take on this responsibility.

What most people can't accept is that creatures like the minotaur most likely had a basis in fact (if not the birth legend). It is one of the best known examples of transhumanism perpetrated by technologically advanced offworld races. There are other illustrations from ancient Sumeria depicting things like man-headed dogs. And this doesn't count all the chimera creatures like the *sirrush* on the Ishtar Gate or that new ugly statue of the Beast at the UN that everyone is up in arms about. Truth is stranger than fiction. But if our genetic scientists are already messing with this type of human-animal hybridization, is accepting this really that far a stretch of the imagination?

There is no God. Professing his existence doesn't say much of anything now, does it. Oooh, I was chosen by a fiction as his servant! Now there's a real ego inflater.

People should be more open to receiving gracefully. Many people can't and suffer the same mindset. It can be overcome with a change of mind - you are worthy of anything that comes to you.

The entire human species is comprised of assholes - ignorant assholes at that. Apes can only blame instincts, humans have abused intellect to make them the ego-driven assholes they are.

I'm not under any stress, I am just watching the victim shit show as your world falls apart, I know why it is happening and am quite sedate over the reason. I am only tossing out lifelines to those who might also want to know. The rest can fuck off.

Perhaps you would be wiser to take things more seriously.

People could fare better if they sought some non-fiction instead of always staying immersed in escapist fantasy.

Say it simply, humans hate being human and want to be anything else and anywhere else than what and where they are. It is a species-wide psychosis that can't be cured.

Everything on this planet is a con job. That is a fact.

There is no devil. Why can't people grow the fuck up?

Shift your perceptions away from the little grey alien narrative and see broader.

All humanity is circling the drain, people are just too stupid to see it or admit it.

I am just stating what is, no tongue in cheek intended. Perhaps you might gain some wisdom from seeing this. It's called problem identification and it might, perhaps, just barely lead to this species finding some genuine solutions to its repetitive insanity.

You have opportunity in being human. It's called freedom of choice, but everyone wants to whine and blame and shame others for their own lack of courage to be more than what they have been indoctrinated to think they are.

Humans can't contend with the intricacies of being human, so they all beg to find some kind of supernatural utopia. Naturally, they also feel that they are entitled to it for no other reason than professing some belief that is their gate pass. Humans are pathetic whiners and beggars.

People need to be concerned *about* the herds, not *for* the herds. There is a distinction.

No one wants to deal with the truth of elite control, it is too big for their tiny little brains to accept. The sanitized condensed and edited lies are more comforting to believe than the ugly larger truths.

To priggish (specifically) Puritanical oriented, mostly American Christians, the nude body is pornographic. It is a real psychosis with that type. One wonders if they all have to shower in the dark or what as much as they hate the naked human body. It really is a sickness.

Tyranny, it is the only evil from which every other evil springs. It is not about good vs evil; it is about freedom vs tyranny.

Tolerance of different ideas is not a general positive human ego trait. That is one of the base problem issues of this species. Everyone wants their freedom, but they don't want to allow it for others. Every ego wants what it wants and fuck anyone who disagrees, particularly if their herd backs them. Tolerance? It is only barely buried resentment.

Some ideas really aren't worth entertaining very deeply. They are usually just curiosities that lead nowhere but keep people happy believing they know something. Most of the conspiracy circus is filled with such pointless curiosities.

Animals have instinct programming to survive, they do not need intellect, which is why they are called dumb animals. Their realm of choice is highly limited to instinct programming. Humanity's intellect capability to make broader choices is what separates them from animals in general.

Humans are generally mediocre because, regardless of how free they believe themselves to be, their reality is dictated to them by narratives created by others and they are too willfully arrogant to perceive how easily they are manipulated by cultural lies and mob enforcement. They are mediocre because they can only think in terms of the herd and pleasing the herd and getting herd approval. They are mediocre because they are generally shallow and superficial, easily driven by ego and manipulable by their emotions and moods. Human intellect is not used to its capacity because humanity doesn't understand itself, nor does it seem inclined to genuinely want to know who and what they really are, nor their place and function in the cosmos. Thus, they are generally dull creatures who think way too much and contemplate little of real value beyond getting their egos gratified.

There will be no human life of leisure once robots replace us. No wireheads intravenously fed while they live in an AI world. If you think humans are useless eaters now, with no need of their labor, humanity is totally expendable to the elite. We will be replaced, end of story.

People are hopelessly addicted to narratives. Their entire lives are shaped by them.

There is no Hell. It is a pacification myth to make people think there is some kind of afterlife revenge for bad people because they are either too lazy or powerless to make the perps pay while they are still breathing. Perhaps if people knew this was just a myth they would stop being complacent in making tyrants and their sycophants pay believing they 'get it' in the afterlife. People do not realize the psychological salve created by this myth and the false comfort and docility it brings to people who are suckered into believing it.

Ah how the defenders justify their fictions.

The college degree is not necessarily the mark of excellence or original thinking, it means the receiver has jumped through all the approval hoops of the indoctrinaires and has accepted coloring within the narrative and institutional lines dictated to them as the playground rules. You are now a qualified parrot. The paper does not endow one with intelligence like the Scarecrow in The Wizard of Oz when he was handed his honorary scroll. It is only an ego bragging right and often not worth the paper it is written on.

Academics and intellectuals are probably more hard-headed than religionists.

If humanity survives its stupidity - which I think is highly questionable at this point. We can only improve ourselves. However much we advance ourselves in these lifetimes, our sentient consciousness takes away with it when the form dies. I prefer to not settle for human mediocrity in this life. The rest of humanity is not my problem. I can only advance me.

We are at the crux of an evolutionary process, but humans don't want to evolve. They only want free handouts from God, the Universe, or aliens or whatever. They refuse to do for themselves in any major constructive capacity. If you are content with what you have, then good lock with that.

There are 7 billion flesh robots on this planet who are not carrying their own slack. If they don't have the courage or wisdom to break the patterns of thought that have controlled humanity's mind as a whole, then the species is going down the shitter.

Only narrative controlled drones are stupid enough to die for a cause - a political ideology or a religion. Freedom is not a cause; it is a state of being that this species knows little about except as a 'cause'. Each ideological herd wants their 'version' of freedom, which always comes with constraints, and they do not want to allow any differing perspectives to have their freedom. Thus, we find ourselves at the point of a species-destructive conflict which may well end in our extinction in the very near future if we don't choose another course. The species is already committing suicide through stupidity and fear with the vax scare. Do you think it is going to get any better if things stay as they always have been? Can humanity choose another path for itself? Right now. it looks pretty grim.

Why is it that people worldwide seek wisdom, yet when they find someone who may know more than them they resent it? Do you have a problem with the idea that perhaps I perceive more than you presently do, but also that you can too if you choose to get over being offended by not knowing what I know? I never said anything about my knowledge being exclusive, anyone can do it if they want to achieve it. Are you just not interested and choose to wander in the squalor of ignorance? Think about this very hard before you answer. That is the choice all humanity is facing at this moment - to continue to wallow in the sewers of ignorance or seek to transcend it. Which do you want? Only you can decide for you, you can't decide for another.

I would prefer to see humanity step up to the plate and become something more than groveling entitlement slaves to gods and governments. Alas, they love their slavery too much to save themselves. They could, they just won't.

If humanity doesn't choose to change itself, we are liable to not be around in a few decades. We will not be the first human species to extinct itself in the history of the cosmos. Stupidity has a price. We are paying it now.

Only sheep need masters. They are only slaves, there to be fleeced then slaughtered.

I don't really care what apologists think. They are only ignorant defenders.

Every human herd is victimized by opposing human herds.

The whole human species is incompetent to do for itself. Whether it is relying on God or government, humanity doesn't have the capacity to rule itself. Hell, most people can't behave themselves civilly without threat of punishment. This cannot be denied.

Our heads are filled with tons of programming that shapes the ego. Most of this programming we refuse to acknowledge as nothing more than beliefs. When we challenge ourselves with the question, 'why do I believe what I believe?', and really start to analyze the reasons why we do with honesty, we discover that most of what we believe that shapes who we think we are comes from outside sources - cultural programming, religion, political perspectives - everything. Whatever beliefs we adopt shape the personality of the false ego. These things create a 'character' that conforms with the narratives we accept as our dictated reality, a caricature of a true individual that we have convinced ourselves is us, when it isn't. Thus, you discover the false ego and put it to rest.

There is no need for a supernatural God at all to fix human affairs that humans refuse to fix for themselves.

Everything humanity believes is part of the Big Lie. Humanity refuses to accept this one major truth.

A 'country' is comprised of its people, and the American people are supernaturally dependent slaves to a pacifist narrative expecting a non-existent God to fix what they refuse to do for themselves. Why the surprise?

Christianity's doctrine of docility set Christians up to be pacifistically bulldozed into the ground believing in non-existent supernatural beings to protect them from the lunacy of the species. This is all humanity's fault, collectively, and there is no God that has *ever* fixed it or will. Begging the skies for succor and relief has never stopped tyranny, but it sure cowed a lot of the population by making them believe it is true.

You can't win an 'intellectual war' trying to convince drones programmed to ignorance and driven by their emotions. Sadly, the drones comprise the vast majority of humans on this planet, so it is a lost battle from the outset. Blind narrative following and apologetics to support herd-accepted deceits will not win the minds of the mindless.

Humanity has always been controlled zombies. It only appears different according to which zombie narrative they defend. It is always 'those people' who are the zombies, never acknowledging our own zombiehood.

You can't expose lies and deceit to people who insist on embracing any part of the lies as their defense and deny they are part of the lies too.

The entire God dependency thing needs to be retired from human thinking. It only provides for victims and those with a glory wish for the afterlife. Beyond that the God concept serves humanity in no positive capacity. It makes them irresponsible slaves to supernatural expectations which simply aren't true. A lie is a lie, and just because it is wrapped in faux holiness doesn't make it less a lie.

The biggest threatened species on this planet is stupid humans.

Monotheism gave us nothing but slavery.

Ignorance has a price and humanity's bill is past due.

The people have no wit to lead themselves. They don't know where to start. They will just choose another 'leader' and step right back into the authoritarian trap they are trying to escape from.

Stupidity and human species arrogance is causing humanity's demise. Good riddance to a species too dumb to grow beyond its ignorance and fantasy escapist beliefs.

Preachers can't be truthful given the product they peddle.

Dump the reliance on the narratives as the 'truthy truth' will reveal itself. It won't so long as you feed the narratives that claim to be truth. Belief isn't truth, it's just the hope that it is.

The healing this species needs is not physical, it is psychological. Wishful thinking and avoiding the bad programming of the ego will not resolve this species malady. If humanity cannot heal its mind the physical form is meaningless. You are watching what incorrect focus on the problem is doing to this species. It is not about joy and bliss and utopia, it is about cleaning your own cognitive and emotional house and dumping your own trash. Anything less only leaves you spinning your wheels going nowhere, placebo effect or not.

This is not a soul test; it is a test of the intellect and emotion programming of the flesh robot and whether this species can pull its head out of its ass and avoid self-extinction or not.

That's the problem with humans, they can't think for or behave themselves without someone giving them instructions. Fact!

Spare humanity from any kind of zealotry.

You can't question God. What does that tell you?

If the 'Father' needs glorifying, he is a narcissist of the worst kind.

Christianity started as a crackpot cult, like it or not.

I can't wait for the disappointment of yet another failed prophecy in the spiritual arena. Nothing ever predicted has happened, they just keep changing the dates and the suckers keep drinking the kool-aid.

Fear porn has been around for millennia. Religions are the worst perpetrators and propagators of it. Shall I mention Satan and Hell? Not that hard to figure out how to mind control the herds.

Contrary to a lot of propagandized UFO beliefs, we do not have a bunch of benevolent alien babysitters buzzing the skies looking out for our interests. The UFO shit was folded into the Lucis Trust disinformation network as early as the 50s and heavily promoted as another hopium ideology ever since.

No one is as awake as their ego makes them believe.

As humanity swirls the drain to possible extinction, I won't be saying I told you so, I will be saying, if anything, you had your chance. You still do, but no one will choose differently.

Same fear narrative for 2000 years. It's old and it's fake.

Gotta love the lengths that all religionists go to to protect their narratives.

The only thing delaying things is human ignorance, its reliance on heroes and hopium.

Only an intellectually prideful individual casts aspersions on what it doesn't comprehend or understand. Poked egos are always full of such aspersions when they feel threatened. Projection is their favored weapon.

Your ignorance of the bigger picture is not my issue to rectify, it is yours.

Afterword

You have been presented with a number of challenging ideas in this volume such as The Actuality and humans being Flesh Robots, to name just a couple. These items and more have been discussed at length in our library of works, the list and sequence of publication follows for those interested.

We are more than what we think we are as a species. We have been shuttled down fruitless rabbit holes of belief for generations, all designed to subjugate rather than elevate our awareness. We were created as a slave race, whether you can accept that or not, and all our systems of belief and institutions of authority have worked tirelessly over the ages to keep us functioning as slaves. When people hear the word slavery, they think in terms of physical bondage. It is few indeed to perceive cognitive slavery, where people are bound by ideologies and religions that keep them believing that they are only 'lesser beings' to some form of God or another.

The psychological slavery in this species is profound and it is the strongest set of shackles that, believe it or not, we place upon ourselves. Unless and until we choose to cast off these shackles that bind our consciousness, the outlook for humanity is not very promising. With billions of people on this planet willing to kill each other and die for their ideological and religious beliefs of all kinds, humanity is on the verge of species destruction. Only the most willfully blind can't see the crisis humanity finds itself in. The ultimate question we must each ask ourselves is whether we want to grow into and understand the responsibility of freedom, or whether we will continue to be tyrannized by narrative ideologies that only serve to keep us subjugated to a false reality of perceptual illusions. This can only be decided by the individual, by you, for yourself. The vignettes in this book are designed to perhaps jar you from your complacency to see that there is something more to be had out of our existence than marching in lockstep adherence to stories concocted by others to keep humanity under control.

When you look around you at the cancel culture, words and their censorship are the weapons in this psychological war, and propaganda from all sides is the orchestra conductor in a world controlled by narratives. This is the true *Matrix* that the film metaphor referred to. You can either remain prisoner to this matrix, or you can break yourself free from the mental illusion gulag. The choice is yours.

The Evolution of Consciousness Series

Book 1

A Philosophy for the Average Man: An Uncommon Solution to a World Without Common Sense by Endall Beall

Book 2

Willful Evolution: The Path to Advanced Cognitive Awareness and a Personal Shift in Consciousness by Endall Beall

Book 3

Demystifying the Mystical: Exposing Myths of the Mystical and the Supernatural by Providing Solutions to the Spirit Path and Human Evolution by Endall Beall

Book 4

Navigating into the Second Cognition: The Map for your journey into higher Conscious Awareness by Endall Beall

Book 5

The Energy Experience: Energy work for the Second Cognition by Mrs. Endall Beall

Book 6

We Are Not Alone – Part 1: Advancing Cognitive Awareness in an Interactive Universe by Endall Beall

Book 7

We Are Not Alone – Part 2: Advancing Cognitive Awareness through Historical Revelations - Endall Beall

Book 8

Advanced Teachings for the Second Cognition by Mrs. Endall Beall

Book 9

We Are Not Alone – Part 3: The Luciferian Agenda of the Mother Goddess by Endall Beall

Companion Volumes to The Evolution of Consciousness Series

False Prophecies, Reassessing Buddha and the Call to the Second Cognition by Endall Beall

Operator's Manual for the True Spirit Warrior by Endall Beall

Spiritual Pragmatism: A Practical Approach to Spirit Work in a World Controlled by Ego by Endall Beall

Revamping Psychology: A Critique of Transpersonal Psychology Viewed From the Second Cognition by Endall Beall & Mrs. Endall Beall

The Common Sense Revolution: Creating Common Ground and Genuine Common Sense – Endall Beall and the Psoyca Crew (2016)

Second Cognition Series

Book 1

The New Paradigm Transcripts: Teachings for a New Tomorrow by Endall Beall & Doug Michael

Book 2

Breaking the Chains of the First Cognition: Tools for Understanding the Path to the Second Cognition by Endall Beall & Doug Michael

Book 3

PSOYCA – Road to the Second Cognition by Endall Beall & Doug Michael

Book 4

The Energetic War Against Humanity: The 6,000 Year War Against Human Cognitive Advancement by Endall Beall

Book 5

The Cognitive Illusion of History: How Humanity Has Been Controlled Through Selective and Biased Historical Reporting by Endall Beall & Doug Michael

Book 6

The Second Cognition Toolbox: Requirements for Advancing Your Consciousness by Endall Beall

Book 7

Firestarters: The Gemma and Endall Transcripts – by Endall Beall and Gemma Beall

Book 8

No Trespassing: Creating a New World Based on Mutual Respect by Endall Beall

Book 9

Psoyca Consciousness by Endall Beall

Companion Volumes to the Second Cognition Series

Understanding Wisdom: A Treatise on Wisdom Viewed from the Second Cognition by Endall Beall

From Belief to Truth – From Truth to Wisdom by Endall Beall

The Psychology of Becoming Human: Evolving Beyond Psychological Conditioning by Endall Beall

Standalone Work: Available for free .pdf download at our website

Clarifying the don Juan Teachings for the Second Cognition: A Pragmatic Reanalysis Without the Mystical Misdirection – by Endall Beall

Beyond Don Juan: Into the Third Attention – The Second Cognition (2019) - by Endall Beall

Consciousness Evolves, Intellect Doesn't: Why Humanity Can't Advance its Consciousness (2020) – by Endall Beall

Find free pdf downloads for these books at the links below, or look for them under the header of Companion Books to the Series at our website https://www.demystifyingthemystical.com/#/

https://www.demystifyingthemystical.com/#/book/17

https://www.demystifyingthemystical.com/#/book/64

https://www.demystifyingthemystical.com/#/book/65

Beyond Second Cognition Series

Book 1

Gutting Mysticism: Explaining the Roots of All Supernatural Belief by Endall Beall (2018) by Endall Beall

Book 2

Religion, the Goddess and the Mind Virus of Heaven: The Deception of Holiness in Human Belief Systems (2018) by Endall Beall

Book 3

Introduction to the Multiverse: The Layman's Guide to the Cosmos (2018) by Endall Beall

Book 4

Facing the Truth: Conspiracy or Plan? 100 Years of Subversive Psychological Warfare Against America by Endall Beall (2018)

Book 5

The No Rules Multiverse: The Endeavor to Repair a Faulty Creation by Endall Beall (2019)

Book 6

Into the Hinterlands: Beyond Second Cognition) by Endall Beall (2019

Book 7

Mission Earth: Advanced Messages for Psoyca Ground Crew – (2020) – Endall Beall

Book 8

Voodoo Reality: The Strangeness of Creation by Endall Beall (2020)

Book 9

The Flesh Robot: The Truth About the Human Computer by Endall Beall (2020)

Book 10
The Flesh Robot – Part 2: Explaining the Nature of the Cosmos and How it is Changing by Endall Beall (2020)

Companion Volumes to Beyond Second Cognition Series

Emotionalism: How the Human Herds are Controlled by Endall Beall (2019)

The Truth About the 'Divine' Soul: The Late Creation of the Concept of Heaven by Endall Beall (2019)

Challenging Philosophy and the Philosophers" Explaining Nietzsche to Philosophical Academia by Endall Beall (2019)

Explaining the Shift in Consciousness: Translating the 'Becoming' book from the New Paradigm Trilogy by Endall Beall (2020)

The End of the World as We Know It: A New World for Advanced Consciousness by Endall Beall (2020)

Facing the Truth – Redux: What the Great Awakening is About by Endall Beall (2020)

Into the Hinterlands Series

Book 1

The New Great Awakening: What People Think it Means and What it Actually Portends by Endall Beall (2020)

Book 2

End Times or a New Beginning?: Humanity's Moment to Evolve by Endall Beall (2020)

Book 3

True Enlightenment: How Humanity Has Gotten it Wrong by Endall Beall (2020)

Book 4

From Dark to Light: A Voice in the Wilderness by Endall Beall (2021)

Book 5

The Actuality: The Process of Life by Endall Beall (2021)

Book 6

The Goddess Who Wasn't a Goddess: The Greatest Conspiracy Scam in Human History by Endall Beall (2021)

Book 7

Normalcy Bias: Why Humanity Can't Advance Itself by Endall Beall and Arch Bramble (2021)

Book 8

The Actuality Field: How Humans Interface with Consciousness by Endall Beall (2021)

Companion Volumes to the Into the Hinterlands Series

The Afterlife: Religion and Spirituality's Psychological Weapon Against Humanity by Endall Beall (2020)

A World in Collapse: Observations from the Outskirts by Endall Beall (2021)

Wisdom. Freedom and Consciousness by Endall Beall (2021)

To Form a More Perfect Union: Government by Responsible Individuals by Endall Beall (2021)

Wisdom for the Brave and Sober Mind by Endall Beall (2021)

New Beginnings Series

To Be Announced

Companion Volumes to the New Beginnings Series

Unpampered Wisdom: Wisdom for the Thick-skinned Individual by Endall Beall (2022)

Upcoming Volumes

The Final Frontier: Can Humanity Mature Into Consciousness? by Endall Beall

The Freedom Factor: Subjective Reality: Infinite Variations by Endall Beall

Integration: Humanity's 'Knowing' Mergence with Consciousness by Endall Beall

For questions or inquiries contact the authors at *http://demystifyingthemystical.com/#/*

Further work by these authors can be found at the Gemma Beall YouTube channel at
https://www.youtube.com/channel/UCN3VfiNrozRSUBi DIR8k9EA

Video podcasts can also be found at our Rumble page at Willful Evolution at the link below

https://rumble.com/c/c-405017

Or through the Gemma Beall Patreon website for subscriptions of $5 per month for access to over 600 video and podcast presentations, and $15 per month for all the videos and an expanding number of educational discussions, chapter previews, blogs and an interactive community forum.

https://www.patreon.com/GemmaBeall/